Ravenous Reptiles

Lynn Huggins-Cooper

W
FRANKLIN WATTS
LONDON • SYDNEY

First published in 2005 by Franklin Watts
96 Leonard Street, London EC2A 4XD

Franklin Watts Australia
Level 17/207 Kent Street, Sydney NSW 2000

Editor: Jennifer Schofield
Jacket designer: Peter Scoulding
Designer: Jay Young
Picture researcher: Diana Morris

Acknowledgements:
Franco Banfi/Bruce Coleman Collection: 14. Jonathan Blair/Corbis: 13. Perry
Conway/Corbis: 16, 20, 22b. Michael Fogden/OSF: 19, 21. Chinch Gryniewicz/
Ecoscene: 17. Philippe Henry/OSF: 11. Daniel Heuclin/NHPA: 5t, 24, 26, 27.
Mark Jones/OSF: 29. Claus Mayer/Still Pictures: 1, 23. National Zoological Park,
©2005 Smithsonian Institution: 8. R. Andrew Odum/Still Pictures: 12. Chris Perrins/
OSF: 18. Fritz Polking/Still Pictures: 28-29b Kevin Schafer/Still Pictures: 10. Roland
Seitre/Still Pictures: 9. ©SA Teamphot Natura/FLPA: 22. Steve Turner/OSF: 15.
A & J Visage/Still Pictures: front cover cl, 4. Adrian Warren/Ardea: front cover r, 6, 7.
Gunter Ziesler/Still Pictures: front cover bl, 5b. ZSSD/Minden Pictures/FLPA: 25.

A CIP catalogue record for this book
is available from the British Library.

ISBN: 0 7496 6095 3
Dewey Classification: 597.9

Printed in China

Contents

Ravenous reptiles

There are nearly 6,000 species of reptile. Although many are harmless, large reptiles, such as alligators, Komodo dragons and gila monsters, are some of the scariest creatures on Earth.

Many of these bigger reptiles are poisonous, and most will attack if threatened. All over the world, stories are told about reptiles that have attacked people and pets – terrorising whole villages.

Fact!

Reptiles are cold-blooded animals that have backbones and scaly skin.

Friend or foe?

Many of the reptiles that people think of as frightening are in fact shy creatures that are not interested in human prey.

But how can you tell whether a reptile is a friend or foe? Are all reptiles dangerous? Is that a log floating past or is it a giant black caiman, sliding closer, ready to snap your boat in two? Read on to find out more about these killer predators. It might just save your life one day.

Dangerous dragons

Komodo dragons are found on the island of Komodo and on other islands in Indonesia.

Their yellow, darting tongues look just like flickering flames. So it is not surprising that fishermen who sailed around Indonesia long ago, brought back stories of very fierce, fire-breathing dragons.

Vital statistics

Komodo dragons are the world's largest lizards. They can grow up to a staggering 2.5 metres long – that is longer than your bed! Males are larger than females and can weigh up to 100 kilograms. Females tip the scales at 68 kilograms.

Record breaker!

The largest Komodo dragon weighed an incredible 166 kg and was as long as most cars at 3.13 m.

How they kill

These fierce lizards hunt by swinging their heads from side to side. They 'taste' the air to find prey by flicking their yellow, stripy tongues in and out. Komodo dragons rush at their prey, killing it with brutal force. They rip off chunks of their victim's flesh and throw it into their mouths.

When Komodos attack

Komodos have sharp, serrated teeth. Their saliva (spit) contains more than 50 types of bacteria. If an animal is bitten by a Komodo, even if it escapes it will die from blood poisoning.

Fact!

Komodos cannot hear high-pitched sounds. So, if you are bitten, they will not hear you scream.

More about Komodos

Baby Komodo dragons

Komodo dragons lay 15–30 leathery eggs that take seven months to hatch. As soon as they are born, the hatchlings scramble up trees to avoid being eaten by adult Komodo dragons.

Greedy monster!

Dr Walter Auffenberg, a scientist working with Komodo dragons, once saw a 50-kilogram Komodo gobble up a 31-kilogram boar in only 17 minutes!

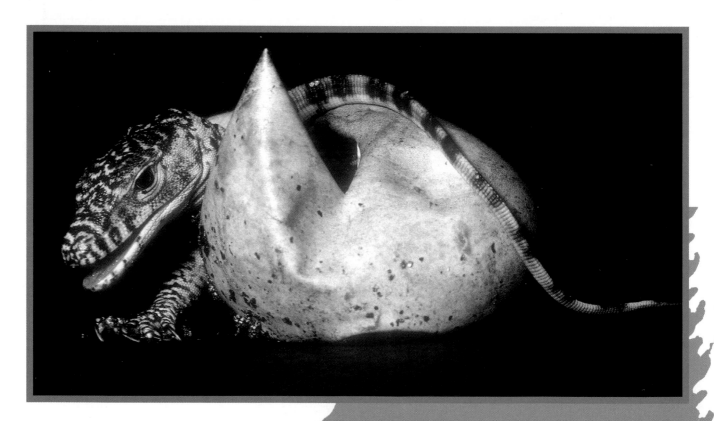

Survival

Today there are only about 6,000 Komodos living in the wild. In 1980, Komodo National Park, Indonesia was created to protect Komodo dragons.

Kraken the Komodo

In 1992 Kraken was the first Komodo to be born in captivity. She was born at the National Zoo in Washington DC, USA. Many of her relatives are now found in zoos around the world.

Real-life story

In 2001, the actress Sharon Stone and the editor of the *San Francisco Chronicle*, Phil Bronstein, entered the Komodo enclosure at the Los Angeles Zoo, USA.

As photographs were being taken, the dragon lunged forward and bit a chunk out of Mr Bronstein's foot. He was rushed to hospital for treatment against the toxins in the lizard's saliva.

Death-roll alligators

American alligators, or 'gators as they are often called, are found in southeast USA. They live only in fresh water such as rivers and swamps.

These fierce beasts can lie dead-still, waiting for prey with only their nostrils and eyes showing – it is easy to mistake them for logs!

Vital statistics

American alligators can reach a weight of more than 270 kilograms and can grow to over 5 metres in length.

In the wild, alligators can live for 50 years. In zoos, they normally live for up to 80 years.

How they kill

American alligators can run for short distances at nearly 50 kph. They use this incredible speed to charge at any unsuspecting animals drinking at water holes, for example.

Alligators attack their prey with their strong jaws and then drag it into the water. Once the animal is in the water, the alligators spin in a 'death roll' to drown their victim.

Encounters with people

As houses are built in places where alligators live, there is more contact between people and these dangerous beasts. Each year, the Florida Fish and Wildlife Conservation Commission (FWC) receives more than 15,000 alligator-related complaints.

Most of these complaints are about alligators being found in backyard ponds, swimming pools and near golf courses. In many cases, if the alligators are left alone, they will move away from people, causing little or no harm.

More about 'gators

Baby 'gators

Female American alligators build nests out of mud and plants. They lay their eggs in the nest and then cover them with debris, such as leaves and twigs. They stay nearby to protect the eggs.

When the babies are ready to hatch, they make noises and their mother digs the nest open. About 80 per cent of the babies are eaten by birds, snakes, raccoons, otters and other alligators.

Fact!

Alligators have about 80 teeth. As they wear down, new ones grow — about 2,000 in a 'gator's lifetime.

Real-life story

In 1977, David Peters and his dog King (below), were swimming in Lake Beulah in Florida, USA. Suddenly, King was attacked by an American alligator.

David was brave enough to rescue his dog but his arm was badly injured. They were both very lucky not to be eaten by the vicious reptile.

Survival

Between 1870 and 1970, about 10 million American alligators were killed for their skins. The skins were made into designer shoes, bags and belts.

Today, American alligators are a protected species. This means that they are protected from poachers by special laws.

Scary salties

Saltwater crocodiles are the world's largest and most dangerous crocodiles. They are found in southeast Asia, Indonesia, the Philippines, New Guinea and Australia.

These fearsome reptiles live in the ocean, sea inlets, swamps and river mouths. 'Salties', as they are known in Australia, can swim for thousands of kilometres.

Vital statistics

Saltwater crocodiles can grow to a staggering 6 metres in length. The average male is about 5 metres long and the average female measures 3 metres.

What's for dinner?

Saltwater crocodiles eat fish, crabs, birds and mammals. Fully grown adult salties have been known to eat animals as large as water buffalo!

How they kill

Just like alligators, these scary beasts drag their prey into the water before drowning it in a death roll. They wait for the body to rot before eating it.

Faster than you'd think

Saltwater crocodiles are aggressive. And while they may look lazy, they can dash out of the water at 70 kph – easily outrunning a person!

Survival

Each year, many baby saltwater crocodiles are eaten by predators. Only 1 per cent of the hatchlings survive to adulthood.

More about crocodiles

Baby saltwater crocodiles

The female crocodile builds a raised nest out of sand and leaves. She lays between 25 and 90 eggs in the nest and guards them fiercely.

The eggs take about 90 days to hatch. When they hatch, the mother carries the baby crocodiles in her mouth towards the water.

Real-life story

In 2001, an eight-year-old girl, Taleesha Fagatilli, was playing in the sea in Australia. A saltwater crocodile grabbed her and tried to kill her with a powerful death roll.

Amazingly, the saltie let go and Taleesha managed to swim away. She was very lucky to survive. In the last 20 years, 12 people have been killed by crocodiles in Australia.

Fact!
Crocodiles have incredibly strong jaws. They use their jaws to crush the skull of their prey.

Greedy gharials

A gharial is similar to an alligator except for its snout, which resembles a duck's bill with a bump on the end.

This terrifying species of reptile is found in the rivers of India, Pakistan, Bangladesh, and Nepal.

Vital statistics

Gharials are not that much smaller than saltwater crocodiles. Average adults grow to about 5 metres long, but there have been reports of 7-metre beasts!

Slithering along

Gharials are great swimmers, but their short, weak legs make them slow on land. To move out of the water, they slide on their bellies rather than walk like an alligator or saltwater crocodile.

Encounters with people

Although human remains and jewellery have been found in their stomachs, Gharials are not as fierce as many alligators and crocodiles.

It is thought that the human remains may have been scavenged from dead bodies. Hindu funerals, held in the areas where gharials live, often end with the remains of the dead person being floated down the river.

Survival

In the 1970s, the gharial nearly became extinct. But areas have now been set aside to protect gharials.

Eggs are collected from the wild and the young are raised in captivity. When they have grown up, they are released back into the wild. More than 3,000 gharials have been released in the last 20 years.

Creepy caimans

Black caimans are large, meat-eating reptiles that spend most of their lives in water.

They are found in freshwater habitats in South America, including rivers, streams, and lakes in tropical rainforests.

Vital statistics

Caimans are the Amazon's largest predator. On average they grow to about 4 metres in length, but giant 6-metre black caimans have been found. They can weigh over 500 kilograms.

Black caimans have a bony ridge over their eyes, and black, scaly skin. Their dark skin helps to camouflage them at night when they are most active. It also helps to absorb heat and keep them warm.

How they kill

Black caimans hunt at night. They leap out of the water to catch prey, but also hunt on land since they are able to run quickly.

What's for dinner?

These fast-moving beasts eat birds, other reptiles and some mammals – they even kill man-eating piranha fish!

Encounters with people

In the lakes of the Amazon rainforest, some people build their houses on stilts.

In the dry season, when the water levels drop, caimans are found hovering near the houses.

Although people can see the caimans' eyes shining in the dark, the reptiles will not attack unless they feel threatened.

More about caimans

Baby black caimans

Female caimans build large nests as big as 1.5 metres across. They lay about 50 eggs in the nest and cover them with leaves and other debris.

When the eggs are ready to hatch, the mother caimans open the nests and help their babies to break through the shells.

Survival

In the 1940s, black caimans were hunted for their skin. This was made into shiny black leather which is used to make expensive wallets and handbags.

Black caiman numbers have dropped by **99** per cent in the last century because of this hunting. As a result, they are now an endangered species.

When caimans attack

Like many other reptiles, black caimans are more likely to attack people to protect their young.

In Ecuador, a group of scientists was catching baby caimans to study them. The huge mother jumped out of the water hissing, and scared off the scientists.

The next night, the scientists went back to the same area. As they caught more babies, the mother leapt out of the water again. She grabbed one of the scientists, dragging him into the water. He was incredibly lucky to escape.

Fact!

Caimans teeth are designed to grab but not rip prey, so they swallow their victim whole.

Poisonous monsters

The gila monster is one of only two species of poisonous lizard – the other is the Mexican beaded lizard.

These small but scary reptiles live in sand burrows in the deserts of Mexico and the southwest USA.

When gilas attack

Although people do not usually die from a gila monster bite, it is incredibly painful. When these beasts attack, they bite hard and hang on tight!

Fact!

Gila monsters can live for months without food. They survive on stores of fat in their tails.

How they kill

The gila monster kills its prey with a strong poison made in glands in its jaw. Its teeth have two grooves that the poison flows down. As the monster bites and chews on its prey, the venom flows into the wound it makes.

Just like Komodo dragons, gila monsters use their senses of taste and smell to hunt. Their forked tongues flick to taste the trail left on the ground by their prey.

Vital statistics

The gila monster is small – it grows up to about 0.5 metres long. Gila monsters have big heads, with strong jaws, and very sharp, slashing claws.

These monsters are covered in tiny scales that make them look as though they have been dipped in coloured beads. The bright colours warn other animals to stay away from them.

Mighty monitors

Mangrove monitor lizards are found on islands in the Pacific Ocean, from Japan to southern Australia.

They were spread among the islands hundreds of years ago by travellers who carried them as a meat supply.

Vital statistics

Mangrove monitor lizards grow to between 0.75 and 1.2 metres in length. Their tails are nearly twice as long as their bodies. Monitor lizards have dark, scaly skin that is covered in small yellow spots.

Fact!

Male monitors do not bite if they feel threatened. Instead, they poo on the creature that threatens them.

Mangrove monitor young

Female mangrove monitor lizards lay up to 12 eggs. These are oblong-shaped and are about 3–5 centimetres long. The young hatch from the eggs in about seven to eight months.

Encounters with people

Mangrove monitors are carnivores. They often attack chickens, with a very nasty bite. To protect their livestock, some farmers trap, poison or shoot the lizards.

How they kill

Mangrove monitor lizards can drop their lower jaw which allows them to open their mouths very wide. Their mouths look as though they are coated in 'lipstick'. The lipstick is actually blood mixed with saliva. It is used to frighten larger predators.

What's for dinner?

These mighty lizards eat mice, rats, insects, crabs and birds. Mangrove monitor lizards that live in towns and cities also eat chicken eggs – sometimes they have even been found to eat foil sweet wrappers!

Clumsy marine iguanas

Marine iguanas live on the Galapagos Islands in South America. When Charles Darwin first saw them, he reported that they were big, disgusting, clumsy lizards.

The film *Godzilla* is about a monstrous lizard that tries to destroy part of New York, USA. To make it look realistic, the film's beast was modelled on marine iguanas.

Vital statistics

Male marine iguanas can weigh an amazing 12 kilograms and can measure up to 1.5 metres in length.

Although they look frightening, marine iguanas are herbivores and feed on seaweed. As they eat, they take in lots of salty water. They have special salt glands between their eyes and nostrils that remove salt from their bodies. When they feel threatened, they shoot the salt in jets to scare attackers!

Survival

The Galapagos Islands are affected by the warm ocean current El Niño. In times of El Niño the ocean water becomes too warm and as a result, the seaweed dies. Up to 90 per cent of the iguana population can starve if there is no seaweed.

Amazingly, marine iguanas can shrink their bodies by 20 per cent so that they need less food to survive.

Marine iguana young

Female marine iguanas lay their eggs in a soft, sandy place on the beach. They lay between one and six large eggs. The eggs can weigh up to a quarter of the weight of the mother.

Key words

Bacteria
Tiny living bugs that can cause extremely harmful diseases.

Burrow
A hole dug by an animal.

Captivity
When an animal is kept in a zoo or in a special conservation enclosure.

Carnivores
The animals that eat only meat.

Charles Darwin (1809–1882)
The British biologist who visited the Galapagos Islands in 1835.

Cold-blooded
An animal that has a body temperature that changes depending on how hot or cold its surroundings are. Reptiles and fish are examples of cold-blooded animals.

Communicate
How creatures 'speak' to one another, or show each other things.

Debris
Bits of plants.

El Niño
A warm ocean current off the coast of South America.

Endangered species
A group of living things in danger of dying out completely.

Extinction
When a group of living things dies out completely, we say it is extinct.

Freshwater
The water found in rivers, lakes and streams.

Habitat
The place where particular plants and animals live.

Hatchling
A reptile that has just hatched out of its egg.

Herbivores
The animals that eat only plants.

Hindu
A person who practises the religion of Hinduism. Hinduism is practised all over the world, but mainly in India.

Livestock
The animals, such as cows and sheep, that are farmed by people.

Mammal
An animal with fur or hair that feeds its young with its own milk. Most mammals give birth to live young.

Poachers
The people who hunt and kill animals illegally.

Predator
A creature that hunts and eats other animals. Komodo dragons and saltwater crocodiles are both predators.

Prey
The animals hunted by other animals for food.

Protected species
A group of animals protected by laws to ensure its survival.

Serrated
When something is sharp, jagged and pointy.

Toxins
Poisons.

Venom
Poison.

Weblinks

www.nationalzoo.si.edu/Animals/ReptilesAmphibians/ForKids/
Loads of reptile activities and games, especially for children.

www.dltk-kids.com/animals/reptiles.html
All the information you will need to make models of your favourite reptile.

www.learningpage.com/freepages/galleries/reptiles.html
Includes fact files, downloadable cut-outs and activity sheets.

www.desertusa.com/animal.html
Features facts and pictures about the reptiles that live in the desert.

www.enature.com
Loads of pictures of reptiles and other interesting animals.

www.sdnhm.org/exhibits/reptiles/index.html
San Diego's Natural History Museum.

Note to parents:
Every effort has been made by the publishers to ensure that the websites in this book are suitable for children, that they are of the highest educational value, and that they contain no inappropriate or offensive material. However, due to the nature of the Internet, it is impossible to guarantee that the contents of these sites will not be altered. We strongly advise that Internet access is supervised by a responsible adult.

Index